EP Second Reader Workbook

I'm _____.

This is my workbook. My favorite books are

_____

_____

_____

_____.

EP Second Reader Workbook
Copyright © 2014 PuzzleFast Books. All rights reserved.

The vocabulary in this workbook is based on, and
used by permission of, Easy Peasy All-in-One Homeschool.
For EP's online curriculum visit www.allinonehomeschool.com

The puzzles and activities in this book may not be reproduced
in any manner whatsoever without written permission from the publisher.
For more information visit www.puzzlefast.com

ISBN-13: 978-1986100601
ISBN-10: 198610060X

Second Edition: February 2018

About This Workbook

This is an offline workbook of vocabulary puzzles and games for Easy Peasy All-in-One Homeschool's reading course for Level 2. We've modified and expanded upon the online activities available at the Easy Peasy All-in-One Homeschool website (www.allinonehomeschool.com) so that your child can work offline if desired. Whether you use the online or offline versions, or a combination of both, your child will enjoy these supplements to the Easy Peasy reading course.

How to Use This Workbook

This workbook is designed to be used as a complement to Easy Peasy's reading curriculum, either the online or offline version. It provides ample activities to help your child master the vocabulary words in Level 2. On any given day, use the Activity List to pick out an activity and have your child work on it. Here's our suggestion:

Use the worksheets with day numbers on the specified days when:
- New vocabulary words are first introduced.
- The online course or EP reader instructs to review the vocabulary words or to play an online vocabulary game.

Use the additional worksheets any time during the course when:
- Your child needs more practice on a specific vocabulary set.
- Your child wants extra activities just for fun.

If your child initially has difficulty remembering all the words, don't worry. The first activity for each vocabulary set is to review all the words and their meanings. The matching activities provided are another a great way to reinforce the meanings of the words in preparation for the more challenging exercises in the workbook.

The solutions to selected activities are included at the end of the workbook.

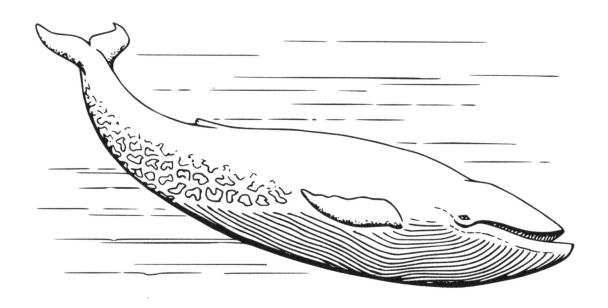

Activity List

Day 21	The City Zoo Vocabulary	9
Day 25	The City Zoo Matching	10
Day 27	The City Zoo Word Search	11
Day 31	The City Zoo Crossword	12
Day 36	The City Zoo Multiple Choice	13
Day 39	Old Mr. Toad Vocabulary	14
Day 46	Old Mr. Toad Matching	15
Day 50	Old Mr. Toad Spelling	16
Day 62	Jimmy Skunk Vocabulary	17
Day 76	Jimmy Skunk Matching	18
Day 81	Jimmy Skunk Word Jumble	19
Day 96	Vocabulary Review Matching I	20
Day 112	Vocabulary Review Matching II	21
Day 117	Vocabulary Review Matching III	22
Day 122	Vocabulary Review Multiple Choice I	23
Day 127	Vocabulary Review Multiple Choice II	24
Day 161	Vocabulary Review Multiple Choice III	25
Day 165	Vocabulary Review Word Search	26

ADDITIONAL ACTIVITIES TO BE USED AFTER DAY 21

The City Zoo Matching 27

The City Zoo Spelling 28

The City Zoo Word Jumble 29

The City Zoo Fill-in-the-Blanks 30

ADDITIONAL ACTIVITIES TO BE USED AFTER DAY 39

Old Mr. Toad Crossword 31

Old Mr. Toad Word Jumble 32

Old Mr. Toad Word Search 33

Old Mr. Toad Word Pieces 34

Old Mr. Toad Fill-in-the-Blanks 35

ADDITIONAL ACTIVITIES TO BE USED AFTER DAY 62

Jimmy Skunk Spelling 36

Jimmy Skunk Crossword 37

Jimmy Skunk Word Search 38

Jimmy Skunk Fill-in-the-Blanks 39

Jimmy Skunk Multiple Choice 40

ADDITIONAL REVIEW ACTIVITIES TO BE USED AFTER DAY 62

Vocabulary Review Word Search 41

Vocabulary Review Crossword I 42

Vocabulary Review Crossword II 43

Vocabulary Review Crossword III 44

Vocabulary Review Word Jumble I 45

Vocabulary Review Word Jumble II 46

Vocabulary Review Word Jumble III 47

Vocabulary Review Word Jumble IV 48

Vocabulary Review Fill-in-the-Blanks I 49

Vocabulary Review Fill-in-the-Blanks II 50

Vocabulary Review Fill-in-the-Blanks III 51

ADDITIONAL ACTIVITIES TO BE USED ANYTIME

Synonyms Matching I 52

Synonyms Matching II 53

Synonyms Matching III 54

Synonyms Matching IV 55
Synonyms Matching V 56
Antonyms Matching I 57
Antonyms Matching II 58
Antonyms Matching III 59
Antonyms Matching IV 60
Antonyms Matching V 61
Synonyms or Antonyms? 62
Homophones Fill-in-the-Blanks I 63
Homophones Fill-in-the-Blanks II 64
Homophones Fill-in-the-Blanks III 65
Homophones Fill-in-the-Blanks IV 66
Prefixes & Suffixes I 67
Prefixes & Suffixes II 68
Prefixes & Suffixes III 69
World Currencies Word Search 70

SOLUTIONS TO SELECTED ACTIVITIES 71

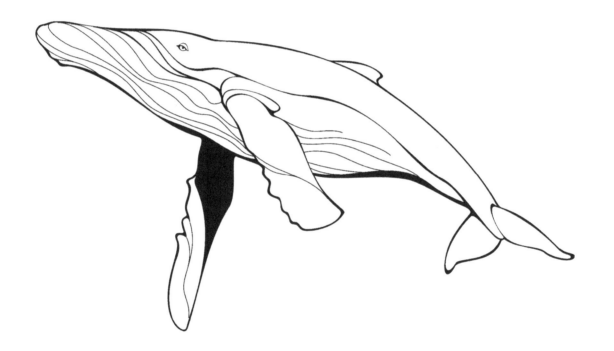

The City Zoo Vocabulary

Day 21

Review and read aloud the words and their meanings.

- emulate = copy someone to try and be as good as them
- wallow = lie relaxed in mud or water
- demolish = knock down a building
- exasperated = extremely annoyed
- intently = with concentration
- disrepair = poor condition
- gleam = shine brightly
- bulge = to be full of
- tirelessly = hardworking
- contented = happy
- slumber = sleep

✓ The moonlight <u>gleamed</u> on the water.
✓ Her pockets were <u>bulging</u> with presents.
✓ She <u>intently</u> looked into my eyes.
✓ She fell into a deep and peaceful <u>slumber</u>.
✓ I was <u>exasperated</u> by his endless grumbling.
✓ The factory is due to be <u>demolished</u> next year.
✓ Classical music made them <u>contented</u> and restful.
✓ The building has fallen into <u>disrepair</u> over the years.
✓ The boy tried to <u>emulate</u> the famous baseball player.
✓ We work <u>tirelessly</u> to ensure the streets are safe and clean.
✓ Pigs do not sweat, so they <u>wallow</u> in mud to cool their bodies.

The City Zoo Matching

Day 25

Can you match the words with their definitions?

disrepair   SLUMBER   tirelessly   demolish
WaLLoW   emulate   gleam   intently
BULGE   contented   exasperated

_____ = copy someone to try and be as good as them

_____ = knock down a building

_____ = lie relaxed in mud or water

_____ = extremely annoyed

_____ = poor condition

_____ = with concentration

_____ = hardworking

_____ = shine brightly

_____ = happy

_____ = sleep

_____ = to be full of

The City Zoo Word Search

Day 27

Find the hidden words and explain their meanings. The words can go in any direction, even backwards! (The solution is on page 72.)

```
G E W F V L W R I D
D R T P J O N N R E
N I U A L L T P E T
A M S L L E G D B A
J V A R N U X L M R
C W N T E L M Q U E
O X L J H P U E L P
N Y O F D M A R S S
T B U L G E V I Y A
E S W G Y K I O R X
N H S I L O M E D E
T I R E L E S S L Y
E C I E S Z A W H B
D M K T D M W M Z P
Q E W B Q H T Q K C
```

bulge

gleam

wallow

slumber

emulate

intently

demolish

disrepair

tirelessly

contented

exasperated

EP Second Reader Workbook · 11

The City Zoo Crossword

Day 31

Across
6. with concentration
7. happy
8. shine brightly
9. extremely annoyed
10. hardworking

Down
1. to be full of
2. copy someone to try and be as good as them
3. sleep
4. lie relaxed in mud or water
5. poor condition

12 · EP Second Reader Workbook

The City Zoo Multiple Choice

Day 36

Choose the word from the definition or the definition from the word.

with concentration
○ wallow   ○ intently   ○ contented   ○ tirelessly

poor condition
○ disrepair   ○ demolish   ○ slumber   ○ exasperated

copy someone to try and be as good as them
○ gleam   ○ bulge   ○ emulate   ○ wallow

exasperated
○ lie relaxed in mud or water
○ extremely annoyed
○ hardworking
○ with concentration

demolish
○ to be full of
○ happy
○ shine brightly
○ knock down a building

slumber
○ sleep
○ poor condition
○ extremely annoyed
○ hardworking

wallow
○ lie relaxed in mud or water
○ extremely annoyed
○ shine brightly
○ sleep

Old Mr. Toad Vocabulary

Day 39

Review and read aloud the words and their meanings.

anxious	=	worried
envy	=	jealous
hastily	=	doing something in a hurry
feeble	=	lacking physical strength
indignant	=	feeling angered or annoyed
amble	=	walking in a slow, relaxed way
smug	=	having too much pride in yourself
scorn	=	thinking that someone or something is worthless or despicable

Peter Rabbit finds Old Mr. Toad

- ✓ Her grandfather is too <u>feeble</u> to work.
- ✓ The rich man was <u>smug</u> and unfriendly.
- ✓ She <u>scorned</u> their views as old-fashioned.
- ✓ Parents are naturally <u>anxious</u> for their children.
- ✓ I <u>hastily</u> finished my homework before the game started.
- ✓ She was full of <u>envy</u> when her sister won the contest.
- ✓ He was very <u>indignant</u> at the way he had been treated.
- ✓ We like to <u>amble</u> through the park on Saturdays.

Old Mr. Toad Matching

Day 46

Can you match the words with their definitions?

- hastily — worried
- anxious — jealous
- indignant — doing something in a hurry
- envy — lacking physical strength
- scorn — feeling angered or annoyed
- feeble — walking in a slow, relaxed way
- amble — having too much pride in yourself
- smug — thinking that someone or something is worthless or despicable

EP Second Reader Workbook · 15

Old Mr. Toad Spelling

Day 50

Can you spell all the words?

jealous

| E | | V | | |

worried

| | N | X | | | U | S |

walking in a slow, relaxed way

| A | M | | | E | |

having too much pride in yourself

| | M | | G |

thinking that someone or something is worthless or despicable

| S | C | | R | |

feeling angered or annoyed

| I | N | | | G | | N | T |

doing something in a hurry

| H | | S | | I | | Y |

lacking physical strength

| F | | E | | L | E |

Jimmy Skunk Vocabulary

Day 62

Review and read aloud the words and their meanings.

shrewd	=	clever
injustice	=	unfair
dignity	=	having honor and respect
thoughtless	=	selfish, thinking only of yourself
acquaintance	=	someone you know, but not really well
impudent	=	not showing respect to someone who deserves respect
admire	=	to have a good opinion of something, to respect someone
suspicion	=	a feeling or belief that someone is guilty or that a certain thought is true

- ✓ The boy who cheated won the game. What an <u>injustice</u>!
- ✓ He was arrested on <u>suspicion</u> of being a spy.
- ✓ She accepted the criticism with quiet <u>dignity</u>.
- ✓ His <u>thoughtless</u> remark made them angry.
- ✓ He is not a friend, only an <u>acquaintance</u>.
- ✓ The <u>shrewd</u> man devised a secret plan.
- ✓ How could you be so <u>impudent</u>?
- ✓ I really <u>admire</u> your enthusiasm.

Jimmy Skunk visits Jonny Chuck's Old House

Jimmy Skunk Matching

Day 76

Connect each word with its definition.

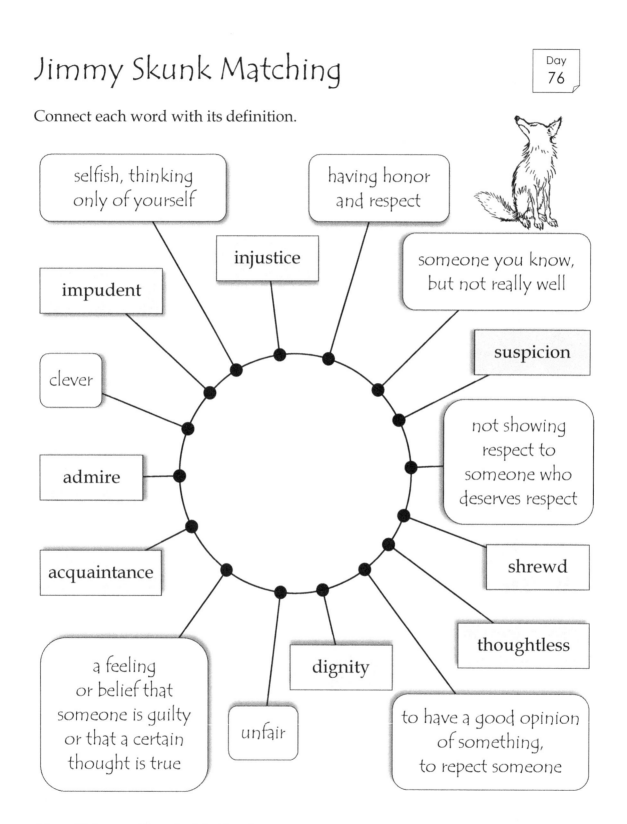

Jimmy Skunk Word Jumble

Day 81

Unscramble the jumbled words.

 having honor and respect

IDITYNG _____

 not showing respect to someone who deserves respect

TINPEDUM _____

 someone you know, but not really well

AQNCTAAUNIEC _____

 to have a good opinion of something, to respect someone

EARDMI _____

 unfair

IINCESJTU _____

 selfish, thinking only of yourself

HTELUHTSOGS _____

 clever

DHRWSE _____

 a feeling or belief that someone is guilty

PSUSIIONC _____

Vocabulary Review Matching I

Day 96

Can you match the words with their definitions?

contented **disrepair** envy intently SHreWd **indignant**
feeble **injustice** dignity aNXIOUS gleam aMBLE

_____ = having honor and respect

_____ = walking in a slow, relaxed way

_____ = angry and annoyed

_____ = with concentration

_____ = poor condition

_____ = shine brightly

_____ = worried

_____ = unfair

_____ = weak

_____ = clever

_____ = happy

_____ = jealous

Vocabulary Review Matching II

Day 112

Can you match the words with their definitions?

tirelessly	sleep
demolish	jealous
slumber	hardworking
bulge	to be full of
wallow	poor condition
envy	knock down a building
emulate	having honor and respect
smug	extremely annoyed
hastily	doing something in a hurry
dignity	selfish, thinking only of yourself
disrepair	lie relaxed in mud or water
thoughtless	having too much pride in yourself
exasperated	copy someone to try and be as good as them

Vocabulary Review Matching III

Day 117

Can you match the words with their definitions?

impudent **thoughtless** **dignity** acquaintance **scorn** Indignant **SUSPICION** Feeble **admire**

_____ = lacking physical strength

_____ = feeling angered or annoyed

_____ = having honor and respect

_____ = selfish, thinking only of yourself

_____ = someone you know, but not really well

_____ = not showing respect to someone who deserves respect

_____ = to have a good opinion of something, to respect someone

_____ = thinking that someone or something is worthless or despicable

_____ = a feeling or belief that someone is guilty or that a certain thought is true

Vocabulary Review Multiple Choice I

Day 122

Choose the word from the definition or the definition from the word.

 worried

○ amble ○ demolish ○ anxious ○ envy

 shine brightly

○ gleam ○ wallow ○ scorn ○ suspicion

 emulate

○ having honor and respect
○ having too much pride in yourself
○ copy someone to try and be as good as them

 feeble

○ lacking physical strength
○ someone you know, but not really well
○ a feeling or belief that someone is guilty

 admire

○ to respect someone
○ jealous
○ thinking only of yourself
○ to be full of

 injustice

○ extremely annoyed
○ knock down a building
○ unfair
○ poor condition

Vocabulary Review Multiple Choice II

Day 127

Choose the word from the definition or the definition from the word.

 jealous

O dignity O injustice O suspicion O envy

 hardworking

O bulge O tirelessly O indignant O thoughtless

 hastily

O feeling angered or annoyed
O copy someone to try and be as good as them
O doing something in a hurry

 exasperated

O extremely annoyed
O doing something in a hurry
O not showing respect to someone who deserves respect

 shrewd

O clever
O thinking only of yourself
O to respect someone
O with concentration

demolish

O having respect
O lie relaxed in mud
O knock down a building
O poor condition

Vocabulary Review Multiple Choice III

Day 161

Choose the word from the definition or the definition from the word.

 unfair

○ dignity   ○ injustice   ○ suspicion   ○ thoughtless

 extremely annoyed

○ feeble   ○ intently   ○ impudent   ○ exasperated

 scorn

○ copy someone to try and be as good as them

○ to have a good opinion of something, to respect someone

○ thinking that someone or something is worthless or despicable

 acquaintance

○ knock down a building

○ someone you know, but not really well

○ selfish, thinking only of yourself

 bulge

○ in a hurry

○ jealous

○ to be full of

 smug

○ having too much pride in yourself

○ feeling angered or annoyed

○ walking in a slow, relaxed way

○ doing something in a hurry

 contented

○ sleep

○ clever

○ happy

○ worried

Vocabulary Review Word Search

Day 165

Find the hidden words and explain their meanings. The words can go in any direction, even backwards! (The solution is on page 72.)

```
T D S F E E B L E D G J B D
N E S D M I H E A R L U E I
A M E C S I N Y D X E T L S
N O L I U B N J Z B A I G R
G L T P O W U T U R M K E E
I I H T I R E L E S S L Y P
D S G J X E V P G N T Q B A
N H U Q N Y S R D E T I J I
I E O F A A K C N H F L C R
K A H Q X Y T I N G I D Y E
C Z T E Z D E T N E T N O C
Y V N E G I M P U D E N T A
```

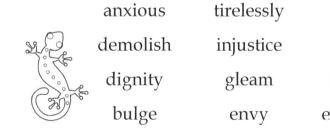

anxious   tirelessly   feeble   thoughtless
demolish   injustice   intently   contented
dignity   gleam   impudent   disrepair
bulge   envy   exasperated   indignant

26 · EP Second Reader Workbook

The City Zoo Matching

Can you match the words with their definitions?

disrepair	happy
slumber	sleep
demolish	lie relaxed in mud or water
wallow	with concentration
contented	to be full of
bulge	poor condition
emulate	knock down a building
intently	extremely annoyed
gleam	hardworking
exasperated	shine brightly
tirelessly	copy someone to try and be as good as them

The City Zoo Spelling

to be full of

| B | | L | | E |

shine brightly

| G | L | | | M |

sleep

| S | | U | | B | | R |

happy

| C | | N | | | | | E | D |

hardworking

| T | I | | | L | | S | | | Y |

extremely annoyed

| E | X | | | P | | R | T | E | |

poor condition

| D | | | R | E | | | I | |

copy someone to try and be as good as them

| E | M | | A | | |

The City Zoo Word Jumble

Unscramble the jumbled words.

sleep
MEBSRLU → _____

happy
NOTCTNEDE → _____

shine brightly
ALMEG → _____

to be full of
EUBLG → _____

hardworking
LRSSYEIELT → _____

poor condition
REISADRPI → _____

with concentration
TIENNTYL → _____

extremely annoyed
PXEATEERSDA → _____

The City Zoo Fill-in-the-Blanks

Fill in the blanks to complete the sentences. Change the word forms if necessary.

emulate   bulge   SLUMBER   wallow   disrepair   gleam
tirelessly   CONTENTED   intently   demolish   exasperated

1. The moonlight _____ on the water.

2. I was _____ by his endless grumbling.

3. Her pockets were _____ with presents.

4. She fell into a deep and peaceful _____.

5. She _____ looked into my eyes.

6. The factory is due to be _____ next year.

7. Classical music made them _____ and restful.

8. The building has fallen into _____ over the years.

9. The boy tried to _____ the famous baseball player.

10. We work _____ to ensure the streets are safe and clean.

11. Pigs do not sweat, so they _____ in mud to cool their bodies.

Old Mr. Toad Crossword

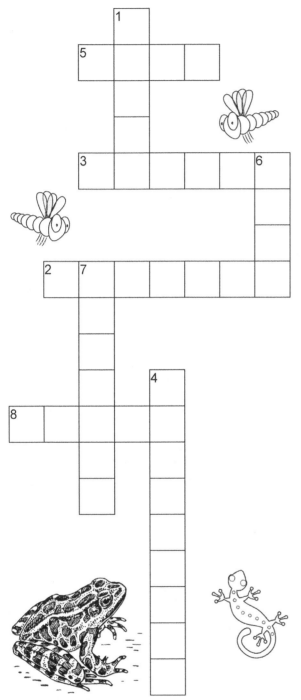

Across
2. doing something in a hurry
3. lacking physical strength
5. having too much pride in yourself
8. thinking that someone or something is worthless or despicable

Down
1. walking in a slow, relaxed way
4. feeling angered or annoyed
6. jealous
7. worried

Here's what Mr. Toad says;
Heed it well, my dear:
"Time to watch for clouds is
When the sky is clear."
- *The Adventures of Old Mr. Toad*

Old Mr. Toad Word Jumble

Unscramble the jumbled words.

walking in a slow, relaxed way

L A M B E → _____

worried

O A I S U N X → _____

jealous

N Y V E → _____

lacking physical strength

E B E E F L → _____

doing something in a hurry

Y L A H T I S → _____

feeling angered or annoyed

D A N I N G I T N → _____

Having too much pride in your self

U M G S → _____

thinking that someone or something or worthless or despicable

S O N C R → _____

Old Mr. Toad Word Search

Find the hidden words and explain their meanings. The words can go in any direction, even backwards! (The solution is on page 72.)

```
E U S Q B S D G U I G X C A
N L K M M J A Y B N T N O W
I A B X U N X E X D E R I F
F S G E X G L F H I Y O R M
R C Q I E B P D Z G T C K B
A V O H M F H B F N E S D Q
O U T A N K V A U A U I F J
S V Y L I T S A H N O B V G
L F W J R D S E P T Y N S A
E N V Y H X L A I V G W C Z
```

amble   feeble   scorn   anxious
hastily   envy   smug   indignant

Old Mother Nature doth provide
For all her children, large or small.
Her wisdom foresees all their needs
And makes provision for them all.
- *The Adventures of Old Mr. Toad*

Old Mr. Toad Word Pieces

Use the pieces below to build words with the given definitions.

worried
| IO | X | US | AN | → _____

feeling angered or annoyed
| IGN | ANT | IND | → _____

doing something in a hurry
| ILY | HAS | T | → _____

thinking that someone or something is worthless or despicable
| CO | S | RN | → _____

having too much pride in yourself
| G | U | SM | → _____

jealous
| E | Y | NV | → _____

lacking physical strength
| B | FEE | LE | → _____

Old Mr. Toad Fill-in-the-Blanks

Fill in the blanks to complete the sentences. Change the word forms if necessary.

anxious   feeble   ENVY   indignant

smug   scorn   amble   hastily

1. Her grandfather is too _____ to work.
2. She _____ their views as old-fashioned.
3. Parents are naturally _____ for their children.
4. He was very _____ at the way he had been treated.
5. She was full of _____ when her sister won the contest.
6. I _____ finished my homework before the game started.
7. We like to _____ through the park on Saturdays.
8. The rich man was _____ and unfriendly.

"Beetle, Beetle, smooth and smug,
You are nothing but a bug.
Bugs are made for Skunks to eat,
So come out from your retreat."
- *The Adventures of Old Mr. Toad*

Jimmy Skunk Spelling

not showing respect to someone who deserves respect

I	M		D			

to respect someone

	D	M			

clever

S			W		

Jimmy Skunk talks to Sammy Jay

unfair

I	N					C	

a feeling or belief that someone is guilty

S		P				N

selfish, thinking only of yourself

T				H	T			

someone you know, but not really well

	C	Q				T		C	

Jimmy Skunk Crossword

Across
6. clever
8. selfish, thinking only of yourself

Down
1. unfair
2. someone you know, but not really well
3. not showing respect to someone who deserves respect
4. to have a good opinion of something, to respect someone
5. having honor and respect
7. a feeling or belief that someone is guilty or that a certain thought is true

Jimmy Skunk Word Search

Find the hidden words and explain their meanings. (The solution is on page 72.)

thoughtless   impudent   INJUSTICE   dignity   admire

shrewd   suspicion   acquaintance   ~~scold~~

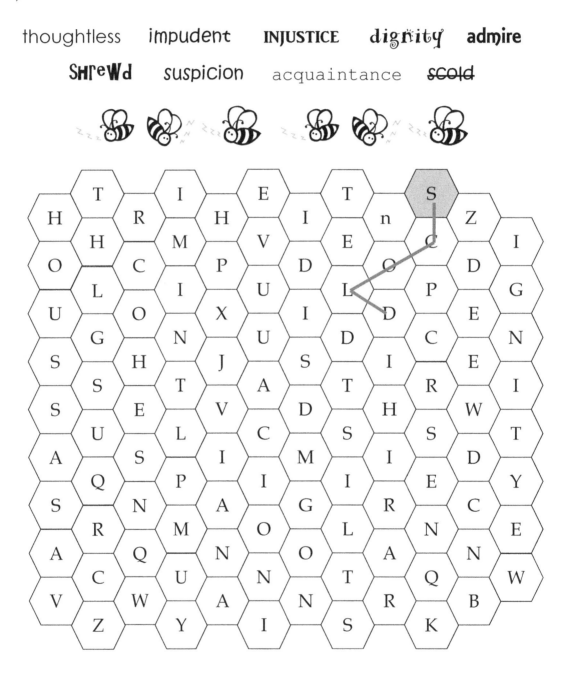

38 · EP Second Reader Workbook

Jimmy Skunk Fill-in-the-Blanks

Fill in the blanks to complete the sentences. Change the word forms if necessary.

thoughtless impudent INJUSTICE dignity

admire shrewd suspicion acquaintance

1. The boy who cheated won the game. What an _____!

2. He was arrested on _____ of being a spy.

3. She accepted the criticism with quiet _____.

4. His _____ remark made them angry.

5. The _____ man devised a secret plan.

6. He is not a friend, only an _____.

7. How could you be so _____?

8. I really _____ your enthusiasm.

Jimmy Skunk bumps into Unc' Billy.

Jimmy Skunk Multiple Choice

Choose the word from the definition or the definition from the word.

 selfish, thinking only of yourself

   O dignity   O injustice   O shrewd   O thoughtless

 acquaintance

O having honor and respect

O someone you know, but not really well

O not showing respect to someone who deserves respect

O a feeling or belief that someone is guilty

 suspicion

O knock down a building

O extremely annoyed

O a feeling or belief that someone is guilty

O not showing respect to someone who deserves respect

 dignity

O jealous

O having honor and respect

O walking in a slow, relaxed way

O having too much pride in yourself

40 · EP Second Reader Workbook

Vocabulary Review Word Search

Find the hidden words and explain their meanings. The words can go in any direction, even backwards! (The solution is on page 73.)

A	E	T	K	C	B	A	S	T	I
S	D	L	O	H	F	C	H	G	E
J	X	M	B	M	H	Q	R	U	T
H	Y	U	I	M	R	U	E	M	A
R	W	L	X	R	A	A	W	S	L
U	E	L	I	T	E	I	D	Q	U
B	U	O	S	T	X	N	V	I	M
N	R	O	C	S	S	T	M	F	E
V	H	C	H	Z	W	A	Y	O	B
U	L	J	Z	A	V	N	H	W	D
D	R	M	L	M	G	C	S	I	H
P	S	L	U	M	B	E	R	T	P
N	O	I	C	I	P	S	U	S	Y
W	N	G	X	K	Q	J	N	Y	K
Y	J	Q	C	Y	R	W	A	Q	G

smug
amble
scorn
admire
wallow
hastily
slumber
shrewd
emulate
suspicion
acquaintance

Vocabulary Review Crossword I

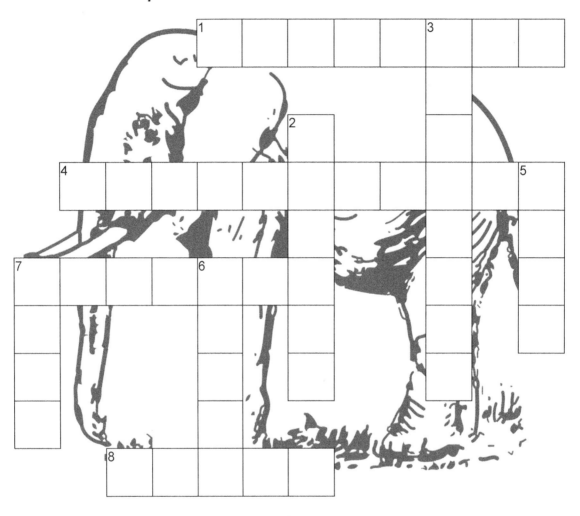

Across
1. knock down a building
4. thinking only of yourself
7. copy someone to try and be as good as them
8. shine brightly

Down
2. clever
3. with concentration
5. having too much pride in yourself
6. walking in a slow, relaxed way
7. jealous

Vocabulary Review Crossword II

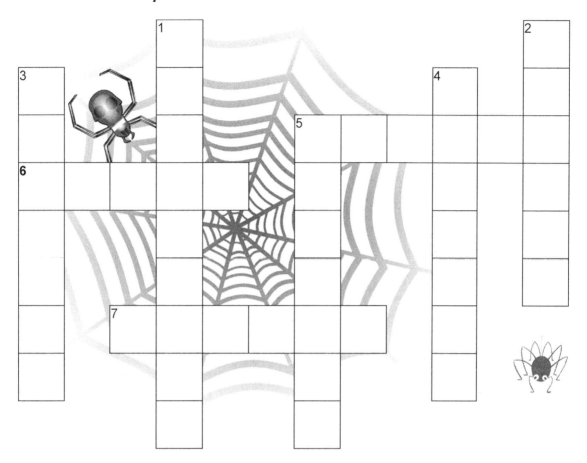

Across
5. to have a good opinion of something, to respect someone
6. thinking that someone or something is worthless or despicable
7. lie relaxed in mud or water

Down
1. poor condition
2. lacking physical strength
3. doing something in a hurry
4. having honor and respect
5. worried

Vocabulary Review Crossword III

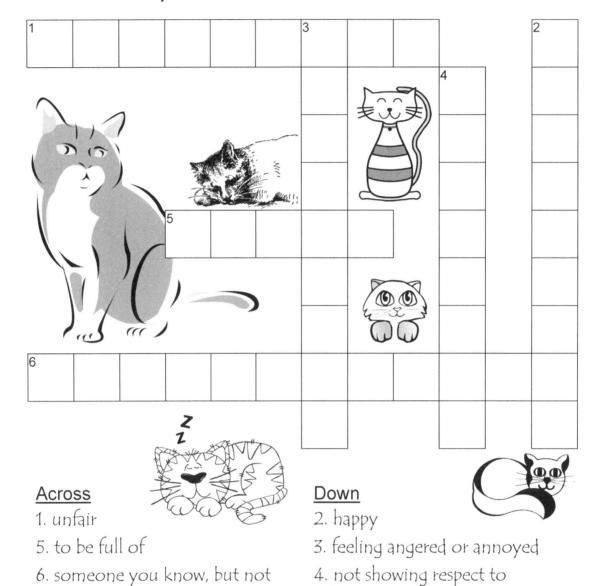

Across
1. unfair
5. to be full of
6. someone you know, but not really well

Down
2. happy
3. feeling angered or annoyed
4. not showing respect to someone who deserves respect

BETTER BY FAR YOU SHOULD FORGET AND SMILE THAN THAT YOU SHOULD REMEMBER AND BE SAD. — CHRISTINA ROSSETTI

Vocabulary Review Word Jumble I

Unscramble the jumbled words to find a hidden word.

doing something in a hurry

LYIHSTA

not showing respect to someone who deserves respect

PUMEINDT

thinking that someone or something is worthless or despicable

CNRSO

copy someone to try and be as good as them

ALUEETM

knock down a building

IHOLESDM

Staying up too late makes me ⭕⭕⭕⭕⭕!

Vocabulary Review Word Jumble II

Unscramble the jumbled words.

a feeling or belief that someone is guilty

SOUCINSIP → _____

thinking that someone or something is worthless or despicable

OCNRS → _____

to have a good opinion of something, to respect someone

MRIDEA → _____

not showing respect to someone who deserves respect

DTPUNEIM → _____

copy someone to try and be as good as them

TLMUEAE → _____

someone you know, but not very well

UIQANECANCAT → _____

selfish, thinking only of yourself

OLUGTTSHSEH → _____

having too much pride in yourself

USGM → _____

Vocabulary Review Word Jumble III

Unscramble the jumbled words.

walking in a slow, relaxed way
L B A E M → _____

lacking physical strength
E E B E F L → _____

lie relaxed in mud or water
W L A O W L → _____

doing something in a hurry
T S Y H L I A → _____

feeling angered or annoyed
N A I N T I N G D → _____

having honor and respect
I I N D G T Y → _____

knock down a building
S E I D H M L O → _____

with concentration
T N L Y T E I N → _____

Vocabulary Review Word Jumble IV

Unscramble the jumbled words.

extremely annoyed
E T A X D S R P E E A → _____

poor condition
I S D I R R E P A → _____

shine brightly
G A M L E → _____

to be full of
L B U E G → _____

jealous
V N Y E → _____

hardworking
T S Y L E R I L E S → _____

worried
N S I U X O A → _____

clever
W S D R H E → _____

Vocabulary Review Fill-in-the-Blanks I

Fill in the blanks to complete the sentences. Change the word forms if necessary.

scorn   thoughtless   impudent   FEEBLE   ADMIRE
exasperated   bulge   ACQUAINTANCE   gleam   slumber

1. The moonlight _____ on the water.

2. Her grandfather is too _____ to work.

3. Her pockets were _____ with presents.

4. I was _____ by his endless grumbling.

5. She fell into a deep and peaceful _____.

6. He is not a friend, only an _____.

7. I really _____ your enthusiasm.

8. How could you be so _____?

9. She _____ their views as old-fashioned.

10. His _____ remark made them angry.

Vocabulary Review Fill-in-the-Blanks II

Fill in the blanks to complete the sentences. Change the word forms if necessary.

hastily disrepair DEMOLISH contented
suspicion shrewd dignity emulate

1. The _____ man devised a secret plan.

2. The factory is due to be _____ next year.

3. She accepted the criticism with quiet _____.

4. He was arrested on _____ of being a spy.

5. Classical music made them _____ and restful.

6. The building has fallen into _____ over the years.

7. The boy tried to _____ the famous baseball player.

8. I hastily _____ my homework before the game started.

Vocabulary Review Fill-in-the-Blanks III

Fill in the blanks to complete the sentences. Change the word forms if necessary.

intently   envy   anxious   tirelessly

wallow   indignant   amble   injustice

1. She _____ looked into my eyes.

2. Parents are naturally _____ for their children.

3. He was very _____ at the way he had been treated.

4. She was full of _____ when her sister won the contest.

5. We work _____ to ensure the streets are safe and clean.

6. We like to _____ through the park on Saturdays.

7. The boy who cheated won the game. What an _____!

8. Pigs do not sweat, so they _____ in mud to cool their bodies.

Synonyms Matching I

Synonyms are words that have the same or nearly the same meaning. Can you match the words with their synonyms? (The solution is on page 73.)

angry	assist
below	purchase
buy	awful
close	mad
help	choose
mix	annoy
business	under
bad	combine
pick	shut
bother	company

Synonyms Matching II

Synonyms are words that have the same or nearly the same meaning. Can you match the words with their synonyms? (The solution is on page 73.)

information	sofa
part	conclusion
find	soil
equal	component
ending	conflict
get	data
couch	same
dirt	locate
picture	receive
fight	image

Synonyms Matching III

Synonyms are words that have the same or nearly the same meaning. Can you match the words with their synonyms? (The solution is on page 73.)

throw	keep
cry	wish
filthy	middle
damp	toss
lid	greedy
save	dirty
fire	sob
hope	cover
selfish	wet
center	flame

Synonyms Matching IV

Synonyms are words with similar meanings. Write a synonym for each word. Use the words from the word box. (The solution is on page 73.)

JOB   **inspect**   **trousers**   *little*   **royal**
eNd   **PRAISE**   **over**   **street**   **earth**

compliment	
above	
finish	
small	
examine	
pants	
road	
faithful	
work	
world	

Synonyms Matching V

Write a synonym for each underlined word. Use the words from the word box. (The solution is on page 74.)

Mad   QUICKLY   tidy   shut   dirty
speak   RIGHt   start   AWFUL   glad

Let's <u>begin</u> the lesson. _____

Your answer is <u>correct</u>. _____

I need to <u>talk</u> with you. _____

I'm <u>happy</u> to see you. _____

Are you <u>angry</u> with me? _____

Please <u>close</u> the door. _____

I ran as <u>fast</u> as possible. _____

The smell is <u>terrible</u>. _____

The room is <u>messy</u>. _____

Your room is very <u>neat</u>. _____

Antonyms Matching I

Antonyms are words that have opposite or nearly opposite meanings. Can you match the words with their antonyms? (The solution is on page 74.)

more		add
forward		female
loose		straight
part		backward
subtract		less
male		whole
harm		tight
visible		sunny
bent		benefit
cloudy		invisible

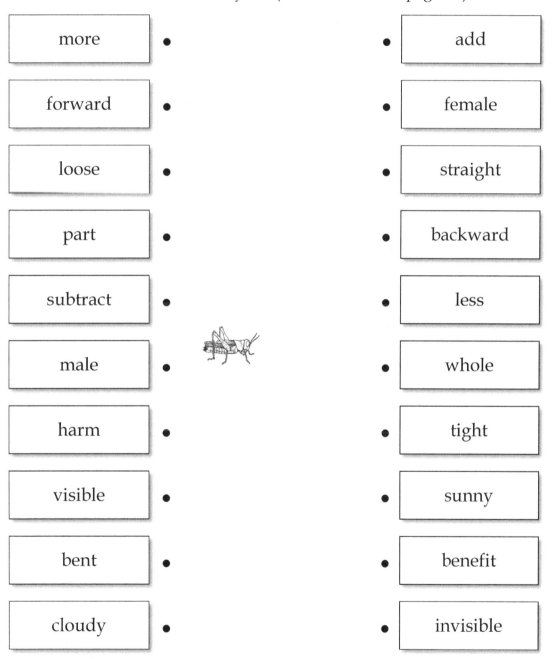

Antonyms Matching II

Antonyms are words that have opposite or nearly opposite meanings. Can you match the words with their antonyms? (The solution is on page 74.)

fall	different
increase	solution
problem	divide
multiply	rise
positive	complex
hire	decrease
similar	negative
follow	rare
simple	lead
common	fire

Antonyms Matching III

Antonyms are words with opposite or nearly opposite meanings. Can you match the words with their antonyms? (The solution is on page 74.)

tall	bland
proud	found
strange	sweet
absent	short
colorful	refuse
against	normal
bitter	ashamed
lost	for
borrow	present
accept	lend

Antonyms Matching IV

Antonyms are words with opposite meanings. Write an antonym for each word. Use the words from the word box. (The solution is on page 74.)

create   dull   win   exit   buy
top   IGNORE   quiet   LONG   unprepared

enter	
prepared	
destroy	
loud	
listen	
lose	
short	
shiny	
bottom	
sell	

Antonyms Matching V

Write an antonym for each underlined word. Use the words from the word box. (The solution is on page 74.)

SLOWLY   WET   BACKWARD   stop   first
west   cold   right   COMPLICATED   cloudy

Let's go to the left.

It's hot today.

The sun rises in the east.

My clothes are dry.

I ran as fast as possible.

This is the last chapter.

The car moved forward.

The question is simple.

The weather is sunny.

Let's begin the lesson.

Synonyms or Antonyms?

Synonyms are words with similar meanings, and antonyms are words with opposite meanings. Tell whether each pair of words are synonyms or antonyms. (The solution is on page 75.)

Word Pairs	Which?
top, bottom	
happy, delighted	
sorrowful, sad	
answer, solution	
calm, windy	
sink, float	
cold, freezing	
tired, exhausted	
full, empty	
far, close	

Homophones Fill-in-the-Blanks I

Homophones are words that sound the same but have different meanings and spellings. Choose the correct homophone for each sentence. (The solution is on page 75.)

ate *or* eight?

I got up at _____ o'clock.

cell *or* sell?

A biologist studies _____ activities.

flour *or* flower?

Cake and cookies are made of _____.

one *or* won?

My team _____ the game yesterday.

sea *or* see?

The blue whale is the biggest _____ mammal.

Homophones Fill-in-the-Blanks II

Homophones are words that sound the same but have different meanings and spellings. Choose the correct homophone for each sentence. (The solution is on page 75.)

---

their *or* there?

They lost _____ toys somewhere over _____.

---

air *or* heir?

Humans cannot live without _____.

---

allowed *or* aloud?

You are not _____ to run in the halls.

---

ant *or* aunt?

My mom's sister is my _____.

---

ark *or* arc?

Noah took two of each animal on his _____.

Homophones Fill-in-the-Blanks III

Homophones are words that sound the same but have different meanings and spellings. Choose the correct homophone for each sentence. (The solution is on page 75.)

piece *or* peace?

Would you like to have a _____ of pie?

whole *or* hole?

He dug a deep _____ with his spade.

deer *or* dear?

_____ feed on a grass, twigs, and bark.

blue *or* blew?

She made a wish and _____ the candles out.

bury *or* berry?

She picked a _____ from the bush.

Homophones Fill-in-the-Blanks IV

Homophones are words that sound the same but have different meanings and spellings. Choose the correct homophone for each sentence. (The solution is on page 75.)

tail *or* tale?

The dog is wagging his _____.

by *or* buy?

I arrived at the airport _____ train.

tea or tee?

Would you like a cup of _____?

here *or* hear?

Can you _____ the noise outside?

weak *or* week?

He was too _____ to stand.

Prefixes & Suffixes I

A prefix is a word part placed in front of a root word. Add a prefix to each word. (The solution is on page 75.)

| re | in/im | mis | un | dis |

_____use   _____cover

_____place   _____view

_____happy   _____appear

_____take   _____lucky

_____play   _____zip

_____agree   _____clear

_____like   _____polite

_____possible   _____honest

_____comfortable _____able

_____capable   _____match

Prefixes & Suffixes II

A suffix is a word part placed at the end of a root word. Add a suffix to each word. (The solution is on page 76.)

| able | ful | al | ion | y |

predict_____   success_____

comfort_____   logic_____

construct_____   reason_____

luck_____   peace_____

help_____   health_____

notice_____   joy_____

subtract_____   wonder_____

thank_____   touch_____

gloom_____   agree_____

care_____   predict_____

68 · EP Second Reader Workbook

Prefixes & Suffixes III

A prefix is a word part placed in front of a root word, and a suffix is a word part placed at the end of a root word. Match the words with their definitions. (The solution is on page 76.)

slower   unable   fearless   joyful   biggest
untidy   worthless   careful   unhappy   disagree

_____ = the most big

_____ = with no worth

_____ = not happy

_____ = without fear

_____ = full of joy

_____ = not clean

_____ = more slow

_____ = you can't do it

_____ = not agree

_____ = with care

World Currencies Word Search

Find the countries and their currencies. The words can go in any direction, even backwards! (The solution is on page 76.)

The United Kingdom uses the Pound.
France, Germany, Italy, and Spain use the Euro.
China uses the Yuan, and Japan uses the Yen.
Mexico uses the Peso, and Vietnam uses the Dong.
Australia and Canada use their own types of Dollars.

Solutions to Selected Activities

Page 11
The City Zoo Word Search

The first letters are marked. Remember that the words can go in any direction!

Page 26
Vocabulary Review Word Search

The first letters are marked. Remember that the words can go in any direction!

Page 33
Old Mr. Toad Word Search

The first letters are marked. Remember that the words can go in any direction!

Page 38
Jimmy Skunk Word Search

The first letters are marked. Remember that the words can go in any direction!

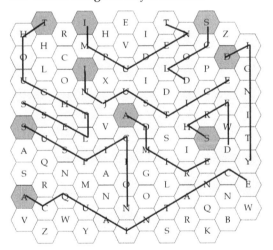

Page 41
Vocabulary Review Word Search

The first letters are marked. Remember that the words can go in any direction!

Page 52
Synonyms Matching I

angry – mad
below – under
buy – purchase
close – shut
help – assist
mix – combine
business – company
bad – awful
pick – choose
bother – annoy

Page 53
Synonyms Matching II

information – data
part – component
find – locate
equal – same
ending – conclusion
get – receive
couch – sofa
dirt – soil
picture – image
fight – conflict

Page 54
Synonyms Matching III

throw – toss
cry – sob
filthy – dirty
damp – wet
lid – cover
save – keep
fire – flame
hope – wish
selfish – greedy
center – middle

Page 55
Synonyms Matching IV

compliment – praise
above – over
finish – end
small – little
examine – inspect
pants – trousers
road – street
faithful – royal
work – job
world – earth

Page 56
Synonyms Matching V

begin – start
correct – right
talk – speak
happy – glad
angry – mad
close – shut
fast – quickly
terrible – awful
messy – dirty
neat – tidy

Page 57
Antonyms Matching I

more – less
forward – backward
loose – tight
part – whole
subtract – add
male – female
harm – benefit
visible – invisible
bent – straight
cloudy – sunny

Page 58
Antonyms Matching II

fall – rise
increase – decrease
problem – solution
multiply – divide
positive – negative
hire – fire
similar – different
follow – lead
simple – complex
common – rare

Page 59
Antonyms Matching III

tall – short
proud – ashamed
strange – normal
absent – present
colorful – bland
against – for
bitter – sweet
lost – found
borrow – lend
accept – refuse

Page 60
Antonyms Matching IV

enter – exit
prepared – unprepared
destroy – create
loud – quiet
listen – ignore
lose – win
short – long
shiny – dull
bottom – top
sell – buy

Page 61
Antonyms Matching V

left – right
hot – cold
east – west
dry – wet
fast – slowly
last – first
forward – backward
simple – complicated
sunny – cloudy
begin – stop

Page 62
Synonyms or Antonyms?

<u>Synonyms</u>
happy – delighted
sorrowful – sad
answer – solution
cold – freezing
tired – exhausted

<u>Antonyms</u>
top – bottom
calm – windy
sink – float
full – empty
far – close

Page 63
Homophones Fill-in-the-Blanks I

eight
cell
flour
won
sea

Page 64
Homophones Fill-in-the-Blanks II

their, there
air
allowed
aunt
ark

Page 65
Homophones Fill-in-the-Blanks III

piece
hole
deer
blew
berry

Page 66
Homophones Fill-in-the-Blanks IV

tail
by
tea
hear
weak

Page 67
Prefixes & Suffixes I

reuse, misuse	recover, uncover, discover
misplace	review
unhappy	disappear
mistake	unlucky
replay	unzip
disagree	unclear
unlike	impolite
impossible	dishonest
uncomfortable	unable, disable
incapable	rematch, mismatch

Page 68
Prefixes & Suffixes II

predictable	successful
comfortable	logical
construction	reasonable
lucky	peaceful
helpful	healthy
noticeable	joyful
subtraction	wonderful
thankful	touchable
gloomy	agreeable
careful	prediction

Page 69
Prefixes & Suffixes III

biggest
worthless
unhappy
fearless
joyful
untidy
slower
unable
disagree
careful

Page 70
World Currencies Word Search

The first letters are marked. Remember that the words can go in any direction!

Made in the USA
Columbia, SC
11 July 2018